My First Riddle

Poets From The South

Edited By Wendy Laws

First published in Great Britain in 2019 by:

YoungWriters®
Est. 1991

Young Writers
Remus House
Coltsfoot Drive
Peterborough
PE2 9BF
Telephone: 01733 890066
Website: www.youngwriters.co.uk

Book Design by Ashley Janson

SB ISBN 978-1-78988-424-1
Printed and bound in the UK by BookPrintingUK
Website: www.bookprintinguk.com
YB0401JZ

FOREWORD

Dear Reader,

Are you ready to get your thinking caps on to puzzle your way through this wonderful collection?

Young Writers are proud to introduce our new poetry competition, *My First Riddle*, designed to introduce Reception pupils to the delights of poetry. Riddles are a great way to introduce children to the use of poetic expression, including description, similes and expanded noun phrases, as well as encouraging them to 'think outside the box' by providing clues without giving the answer away immediately. Some pupils were given a series of riddle templates to choose from, giving them a framework within which to shape their ideas.

Their answers could be whatever or whoever their imaginations desired; from people to places, animals to objects, food to seasons. All of us here at Young Writers believe in the importance of inspiring young children to produce creative writing, including poetry, and we feel that seeing their own riddles in print will ignite that spark of creativity.

We hope you enjoy riddling your way through this book as much as we enjoyed reading all the entries.

CONTENTS

St Michael's CE Primary School, Sunninghill

Waddesdon Village Primary School, Waddesdon

Waterside Academy, Rowans

THE RIDDLES

Oak Class' First Riddle

What could it be?
Follow the clues and see.

It looks like **glass and is grey.**
It sounds like ***dub, dub, pitter-patter, plip-plop, drip-drop, splish, splash*** **and thunder.**
It smells like **water and mud.**
It feels **soft and wet.**
It tastes like **cold water.**

Have you guessed what it could be?
Look below and you will see,
It is...

Answer: **Rain.**

Oak Class (5)

Chawton CE Primary School, Chawton

George's First Riddle

What could it be?
Follow the clues and see.

It looks like **a man.**
It sounds like **silence.**
It smells like **rubber.**
It feels **smooth.**
It tastes like... **you can't eat it.**

Have you guessed what it could be?
Look below and you will see,
It is...

Answer: **Stretch Armstrong (a figure).**

George Tsigarides (5)
Chawton CE Primary School, Chawton

Jorja-May's First Riddle

Who could she be?
Follow the clues and see.

She looks like **a princess.**
She sounds like **sprinkles.**
She smells like **ice.**
She feels **hard and soft.**
she tastes like **iced lemon.**

Have you guessed who she could be?
Look below and you will see,
She is...

Answer: **Elsa.**

Jorja-May Smith (5)

Chawton CE Primary School, Chawton

Freyja's First Riddle

What could it be?
Follow the clues and see.

It looks like **white sparkles.**
It sounds like **a crunch.**
It smells like **yoghurt.**
It feels **soft and crunchy.**
It tastes like **water.**

Have you guessed what it could be?
Look below and you will see,
It is...

Answer: **Snow.**

Freyja Davies (4)
Chawton CE Primary School, Chawton

Reece's First Riddle

What could it be?
Follow the clues and see.

It looks **big**.
It sounds like ***chug***.
It smells like **nothing**.
It feels **soft (seats inside)**.
It tastes like **yucky**.

Have you guessed what it could be?
Look below and you will see,
It is...

Answer: **A rally car.**

Reece Williams (4)
Chawton CE Primary School, Chawton

Sophie's First Riddle

What could it be?
Follow the clues and see.

It looks like **fur**.
It sounds like ***owoo!***
It smells like **skin**.
It feels **hairy**.
It tastes **disgusting**.

Have you guessed what it could be?
Look below and you will see,
It is...

Answer: **A werewolf**.

Sophie Blythe (5)
Chawton CE Primary School, Chawton

Nathan's First Riddle

This is my riddle about an amazing animal.
What could it be?
Follow the clues to see!

This animal has **fur** on its body,
And its colours are **brown and grey**.
This animal has **big** feet,
It likes **lots of grass** to eat.
Australia, in the outback, is where it lives,
Its favourite thing to do is **jumping**.
This animal has **pointy** ears,
It makes **hissing and growling** sounds for
you to hear.

Are you an animal whizz?
Have you guessed what it is?
It is...

Answer: **A wallaby.**

Nathan Lewis Emmons (5)
Lochinver House School, Little Heath

Milan's First Riddle

This is my riddle about an amazing animal.
What could it be?
Follow the clues to see!

This animal has **spots** on its body,
And its colours are **white and black**.
This animal has **paws as** feet,
It likes **dog food** to eat.
A dog house is where it lives,
Its favourite thing to do is **scratch and play**.
This animal has **pointy** ears,
It makes **barking** sounds for you to hear.

Are you an animal whizz?
Have you guessed what it is?
It is...

Answer: **A Dalmatian puppy.**

Milan Bansal (5)
Lochinver House School, Little Heath

Hugo's First Riddle

This is my riddle about an amazing animal.
What could it be?
Follow the clues to see!

This animal has **long fur** on its body,
And its colour is **light brown**.
This animal has **three-toed** feet,
It likes **leaves** to eat.
Latin America is where it lives,
Its favourite thing to do is **move slowly**.
This animal has **tiny** ears,
It makes **squeaky** sounds for you to hear.

Are you an animal whizz?
Have you guessed what it is?
It is...

Answer: **A three-toed sloth.**

Hugo Maximilian Stern (4)
Lochinver House School, Little Heath

Kyan's First Riddle

This is my riddle about an amazing animal.
What could it be?
Follow the clues to see!

This animal has **pink feathers** on its body,
And its colour is **pink.**
This animal has **two** feet,
It likes **algae and shrimp** to eat.
By lakes is where it lives,
Its favourite thing to do is **to stand on one leg.**
This animal has **two** ears,
It makes **squawk** sounds for you to hear.

Are you an animal whizz?
Have you guessed what it is?
It is...

Answer: **A flamingo.**

Kyan Thankar (4)
Lochinver House School, Little Heath

Sebastian's First Riddle

This is my riddle about an amazing animal.
What could it be?
Follow the clues to see!

This animal has **skin** on its body,
And its colour is **green**.
This animal has **zero** feet,
It likes **mice** to eat.
The jungle is where it lives,
Its favourite thing to do is **curl up and sleep**.
This animal has **no** ears,
It makes **ssssss** sounds for you to hear.

Are you an animal whizz?
Have you guessed what it is?
It is...

Answer: **A snake.**

Sebastian Shah (4)
Lochinver House School, Little Heath

Matthew's First Riddle

This is my riddle about an amazing animal.
What could it be?
Follow the clues to see!

This animal has **barnacles** on its body,
And its colour is **blue**.
This animal has **no** feet,
It likes **small fish** to eat.
The ocean is where it lives,
Its favourite thing to do is **to sing**.
This animal has **hidden** ears,
It makes **splashing** sounds for you to hear.

Are you an animal whizz?
Have you guessed what it is?
It is...

Answer: **A blue whale.**

Matthew Joseph Gleeson (5)
Lochinver House School, Little Heath

Harvey's First Riddle

This is my riddle about an amazing animal.
What could it be?
Follow the clues to see!

This animal has **spots** on its body,
And its colour is **yellow**.
This animal has **four** feet,
It likes **wildebeest** to eat.
The desert is where it lives,
Its favourite thing to do is **hunt**.
This animal has **small, round** ears,
It makes **growl** sounds for you to hear.

Are you an animal whizz?
Have you guessed what it is?
It is...

Answer: **A cheetah.**

Harvey Lee (4)
Lochinver House School, Little Heath

Michael's First Riddle

This is my riddle about an amazing animal.
What could it be?
Follow the clues to see!

This animal has **spots** on its body,
And its colours are **yellow and black.**
This animal has **four** feet,
It likes **meat** to eat.
Africa is where it lives,
Its favourite thing to do is **racing**.
This animal has **two** ears,
It makes **roar, roar** sounds for you to hear.

Are you an animal whizz?
Have you guessed what it is?
It is...

Answer: **A cheetah.**

Michael Yang (4)

Lochinver House School, Little Heath

Ethan's First Riddle

This is my riddle about an amazing animal.
What could it be?
Follow the clues to see!

This animal has **fur** on its body,
And its colour is **yellow.**
This animal has **big paws for** feet,
It likes **meat** to eat.
Africa is where it lives,
Its favourite thing to do is **to chase animals.**
This animal has **little** ears,
It makes **roar** sounds for you to hear.

Are you an animal whizz?
Have you guessed what it is?
It is...

Answer: **A lion.**

Ethan Melzack (5)
Lochinver House School, Little Heath

Albert's First Riddle

This is my riddle about an amazing animal.
What could it be?
Follow the clues to see!

This animal has **black spots** on its body,
And its colours are **black and white**.
This animal has **hooved** feet,
It likes **grass** to eat.
A barn is where it lives,
Its favourite thing to do is **eat**.
This animal has **big** ears,
It makes **moo** sounds for you to hear.

Are you an animal whizz?
Have you guessed what it is?
It is...

Answer: **A cow**.

Albert Anderson (4)
Lochinver House School, Little Heath

Daniel's First Riddle

This is my riddle about an amazing animal.
What could it be?
Follow the clues to see!

This animal has **a pattern** on its body,
And its colour is **orange**.
This animal has **a long neck**,
It likes **plants** to eat.
Africa is where it lives,
Its favourite thing to do is **eat**.
This animal has **little** ears,
It makes **humming** sounds for you to hear.

Are you an animal whizz?
Have you guessed what it is?
It is...

Answer: **A giraffe.**

Daniel John Huxley (4)
Lochinver House School, Little Heath

Kore's First Riddle

This is my riddle about an amazing animal.
What could it be?
Follow the clues to see!

This animal has **fur** on its body,
And its colours are **gold and brown**.
This animal has **four** feet,
It likes **meat** to eat.
The jungle is where it lives,
Its favourite thing to do is **hunt**.
This animal has **two** ears,
It makes **roaring** sounds for you to hear.

Are you an animal whizz?
Have you guessed what it is?
It is...

Answer: **A lion**.

Kore Omidiji (4)
Lochinver House School, Little Heath

Blake's First Riddle

This is my riddle about an amazing animal.
What could it be?
Follow the clues to see!

This animal has **fur** on its body,
And its colour is **yellow**.
This animal has **four** feet,
It likes **animals** to eat.
Africa is where it lives,
Its favourite thing to do is **hunt**.
This animal has **two** ears,
It makes **roaring** sounds for you to hear.

Are you an animal whizz?
Have you guessed what it is?
It is...

Answer: **A lion.**

Blake Jackson (4)
Lochinver House School, Little Heath

Emilio's First Riddle

What could it be?
Follow the clues and see.

It looks like **a full moon.**
It sounds like **clanging bells.**
It smells like **fresh soap.**
It feels like **smooth ice.**
It tastes like **hard stone.**

Have you guessed what it could be?
Look below and you will see,
It is...

Answer: ***A plate.***

Emilio Abad Gardner (4)
Lochinver House School, Little Heath

Nathaniel's First Riddle

What could it be?
Follow the clues and see.

It looks like **bright colours**.
It sounds like **bangs and crashes.**
It smells like **smoke**.
It feels **hot**.
It tastes like **explosions**.

Have you guessed what it could be?
Look below and you will see,
It is...

Answer: ***A firework.***

Nathaniel Inglis (5)
Lochinver House School, Little Heath

Maurice's First Riddle

What could it be?
Follow the clues and see.

It looks like **a white blanket.**
It sounds like **shivering.**
It smells like **winter.**
It feels like **powdery sugar.**
It tastes like **ice.**

Have you guessed what it could be?
Look below and you will see,
It is...

Answer: Snow.

Maurice Doggett (4)
Lochinver House School, Little Heath

Drake's First Riddle

What could it be?
Follow the clues and see.

It looks like **a person**.
It sounds like **winter**.
It smells like **a carrot**.
It feels like **ice**.
It tastes like **water**.

Have you guessed what it could be?
Look below and you will see,
It is...

Answer: **A snowman.**

Drake John Ross Bunce (4)
Lochinver House School, Little Heath

Noah's First Riddle

What could it be?
Follow the clues and see.

It looks like **the sky**.
It sounds like **roaring**.
It smells like **freshness**.
It feels like **water**.
It tastes like **salt**.

Have you guessed what it could be?
Look below and you will see,
It is...

Answer: ***The sea.***

Noah Dar (5)
Lochinver House School, Little Heath

Sebastian's First Riddle

What could it be?
Follow the clues and see.

It looks **small and round**.
It sounds like **crunchy balls**.
It smells **buttery**.
It feels **bumpy**.
It tastes **sweet**.

Have you guessed what it could be?
Look below and you will see,
It is...

Answer: **Popcorn**.

Sebastian Fuller (5)
Lochinver House School, Little Heath

Elodie's First Riddle

What could it be?
Follow the clues and see.

It looks like **a little fluffy cloud.**
It sounds like ***squeak, squeak.***
It smells like **hay.**
It feels like **fluffiness.**
It tastes like **mini biscuits.**

Have you guessed what it could be?
Look below and you will see,
It is...

Answer: **A hamster.**

Elodie Reay (4)
Long Crendon School, Long Crendon

Luella's First Riddle

What could it be?
Follow the clues and see.

It looks like **colourful glitter**.
It sounds like ***pitter-patter.***
It smells like **water**.
It feels like **the sun and rain**.
It tastes like **Smarties**.

Have you guessed what it could be?
Look below and you will see,
It is...

Answer: **A rainbow.**

Luella Evelyn Rose Walters (4)
Long Crendon School, Long Crendon

Annabel's First Riddle

Who could he be?
Follow the clues and see.

He looks **cuddly**.
He sounds like ***waa, waa.***
He smells like **baby lotion**.
He feels **soft and smooth**.
He tastes like **sicky milk**.

Have you guessed who he could be?
Look below and you will see,
He is...

Answer: ***My brother, Arthur.***

Annabel McMichael (4)
Long Crendon School, Long Crendon

Alice's First Riddle

What could it be?
Follow the clues and see.

It looks like **a ball of fluff.**
It sounds like **a screech.**
It smells like **sawdust.**
It feels like **soft cotton wool.**
It tastes like **bones.**

Have you guessed what it could be?
Look below and you will see,
It is...

Answer: **A gerbil.**

Alice Hutt (5)
Long Crendon School, Long Crendon

Aurelia's First Riddle

What could it be?
Follow the clues and see.

It looks like **flower petals**.
It sounds like ***flutter.***
It smells **beautiful**.
It feels **soft**.
It tastes like **nectar**.

Have you guessed what it could be?
Look below and you will see,
It is...

Answer: ***A butterfly.***

Aurelia Wong (5)
Long Crendon School, Long Crendon

Betsy's First Riddle

What could it be?
Follow the clues and see.

It looks like **a big creature**.
It sounds like ***neigh***.
It smells like **a stable**.
It feels like **velvet**.
It tastes like **carrots**.

Have you guessed what it could be?
Look below and you will see,
It is...

Answer: **A horse**.

Betsy Barr (5)

Long Crendon School, Long Crendon

Rafe's First Riddle

What could it be?
Follow the clues and see.

It looks like **a furry blob**.
It sounds like **a singing yap**.
It smells like **bones**.
It feels like **softness**.
It tastes like **hot dogs**.

Have you guessed what it could be?
Look below and you will see,
It is...

Answer: **A dog.**

Rafe Kerstein (4)
Long Crendon School, Long Crendon

Annalise's First Riddle

What could it be?
Follow the clues and see.

It looks like **an oval**.
It sounds like ***crack***.
It smells like **chocolate**.
It feels **cold**.
It tastes **yummy**.

Have you guessed what it could be?
Look below and you will see,
It is...

Answer: **An Easter egg**.

Annalise Honour (5)
Long Crendon School, Long Crendon

Scarlett's First Riddle

What could it be?
Follow the clues and see.

It looks **fluffy**.
It sounds like ***squeak***.
It smells like **hay**.
It feels **furry**.
It tastes like **corn**.

Have you guessed what it could be?
Look below and you will see,
It is...

Answer: **A hamster**.

Scarlett Helen Ryan (4)
Long Crendon School, Long Crendon

Tommy's First Riddle

What could it be?
Follow the clues and see.

It looks **blue**.
It sounds like ***drip.***
It smells like **nothing**.
It feels **wet**.
It tastes like **sugar**.

Have you guessed what it could be?
Look below and you will see,
It is...

Answer: **Water**.

Tommy Eaglestone (4)
Long Crendon School, Long Crendon

Zak's First Riddle

What could it be?
Follow the clues and see.

It looks **wet**.
It sounds like ***blub***.
It smells **stinky**.
It feels **slimy**.
It tastes **fishy**.

Have you guessed what it could be?
Look below and you will see,
It is...

Answer: **A fish**.

Zak Morgan (4)
Long Crendon School, Long Crendon

Chloe's First Riddle

This is my riddle about an amazing animal.
What could it be?
Follow the clues to see!

This animal has **a shell** on its body,
And its colours are **brown and black.**
This animal has **four** feet,
It likes **lettuce and cucumber** to eat.
Hot countries are where it lives,
Its favourite things to do are **eat and sleep.**
This animal has **no** ears,
It makes **chomping** sounds for you to hear.

Are you an animal whizz?
Have you guessed what it is?
It is...

Answer: **A tortoise.**

Chloe Parkes (4)
Manorcroft Primary School, Egham

Krithik Moorthy's First Riddle

This is my riddle about an amazing animal.
What could it be?
Follow the clues to see!

This animal has **a long tail** on its body,
And its colour is **black**.
This animal has **big** feet,
It likes **banana tree leaves** to eat.
The jungle is where it lives,
Its favourite thing to do is **play in water**.
This animal has **long** ears,
It makes ***pawoo, pawoo, pawoo*** sounds for you to hear.

Are you an animal whizz?
Have you guessed what it is?

It is...

Answer: **An elephant.**

Krithik Moorthy (5)

Manorcroft Primary School, Egham

Yasemin's First Riddle

This is my riddle about an amazing animal.
What could it be?
Follow the clues to see!

This animal has **wool** on its body,
And its colours are **white and black.**
This animal has **four** feet,
It likes **grass** to eat.
The farm is where it lives,
Its favourite thing to do is **to eat grass and bask in the sun.**
This animal has **two** ears,
It makes **baa-baa** sounds for you to hear.

Are you an animal whizz?
Have you guessed what it is?
It is...

Answer: **A sheep.**

Yasemin Papathanasiou (4)
Manorcroft Primary School, Egham

Isabella's First Riddle

This is my riddle about an amazing animal.
What could it be?
Follow the clues to see!

This animal has **a fluffy tail** on its body,
And its colour is **white**.
This animal has **four** feet,
It likes **fruit and vegetables** to eat.
Holes and burrows are where it lives,
Its favourite thing to do is **hop around**.
This animal has **big** ears,
It makes **squeaky** sounds for you to hear.

Are you an animal whizz?
Have you guessed what it is?
It is...

Answer: **A bunny**.

Isabella Dean (4)
Manorcroft Primary School, Egham

Toby's First Riddle

This is my riddle about an amazing animal.
What could it be?
Follow the clues to see!

This animal has **spikes** on its body,
And its colour is **brown.**
This animal has **claw** feet,
It likes **insects** to eat.
The forest is where it lives,
Its favourite thing to do is **play with balls**.
This animal has **smooth** ears,
It makes ***huff, huff*** sounds for you to hear.

Are you an animal whizz?
Have you guessed what it is?
It is...

Answer: **A hedgehog.**

Tobias Henry Anthony Howard (5)
Manorcroft Primary School, Egham

Alistair's First Riddle

This is my riddle about an amazing animal.
What could it be?
Follow the clues to see!

This animal has **stripes** on its body,
And its colours are **black and white**.
This animal has **four** feet,
It likes **grass** to eat.
Africa and in the zoo is where it lives,
Its favourite thing to do is **eat grass**.
This animal has **pointy** ears,
It makes **horsey** sounds for you to hear.

Are you an animal whizz?
Have you guessed what it is?
It is...

Answer: **A zebra.**

Alistair Foot (4)
Manorcroft Primary School, Egham

Cara's First Riddle

This is my riddle about an amazing animal.
What could it be?
Follow the clues to see!

This animal has **humps** on its body,
And its colour is **brown**.
This animal has **four** feet,
It likes **grass** to eat.
The desert is where it lives,
Its favourite thing to do is **play in the sand**.
This animal has **two** ears,
It makes ***rrrrrrh*** sounds for you to hear.

Are you an animal whizz?
Have you guessed what it is?
It is...

Answer: **A camel.**

Cara Naraine (4)
Manorcroft Primary School, Egham

Valentina's First Riddle

This is my riddle about an amazing animal.
What could it be?
Follow the clues to see!

This animal has **white whiskers** on its body,
And its colour is **black.**
This animal has **four** feet,
It likes **fish** to eat.
Battersea is where it lives,
Its favourite thing to do is **play with a ball.**
This animal has **two** ears,
It makes **miaowing** sounds for you to hear.

Are you an animal whizz?
Have you guessed what it is?
It is...

Answer: **A cat.**

Valentina Cristiano (5)
Manorcroft Primary School, Egham

Kavi's First Riddle

This is my riddle about an amazing animal.
What could it be?
Follow the clues to see!

This animal has **hair** on its body,
And its colour is **black**.
This animal has **four** feet,
It likes **an apple** to eat.
A grass field is where it lives,
Its favourite thing to do is **galloping**.
This animal has **two** ears,
It makes **neighing** sounds for you to hear.

Are you an animal whizz?
Have you guessed what it is?
It is...

Answer: **A horse.**

Kavi Sohi (4)
Manorcroft Primary School, Egham

Henry's First Riddle

This is my riddle about an amazing animal.
What could it be?
Follow the clues to see!

This animal has **a tail** on its body,
And its colour is **blue**.
This animal has **no** feet,
It likes **krill** to eat.
The ocean is where it lives,
Its favourite thing to do is **sleep**.
This animal has **two** ears,
It makes **wailing** sounds for you to hear.

Are you an animal whizz?
Have you guessed what it is?
It is...

Answer: **A blue whale**.

Henry Emmanuel Masih (4)
Manorcroft Primary School, Egham

Benjamin's First Riddle

This is my riddle about an amazing animal.
What could it be?
Follow the clues to see!

This animal has **wool** on its body,
And its colour is **white.**
This animal has **four** feet,
It likes **grass** to eat.
The farm is where it lives,
Its favourite thing to do is **eat.**
This animal has **two** ears,
It makes **baaing** sounds for you to hear.

Are you an animal whizz?
Have you guessed what it is?
It is...

Answer: **A sheep.**

Benjamin Moore (4)
Manorcroft Primary School, Egham

Sienna's First Riddle

This is my riddle about an amazing animal.
What could it be?
Follow the clues to see!

This animal has **stripes** on its body,
And its colours are **black and white**.
This animal has **four** feet,
It likes **grass** to eat.
A field is where it lives,
Its favourite thing to do is **run**.
This animal has **two** ears.

Are you an animal whizz?
Have you guessed what it is?
It is...

Answer: **A zebra.**

Sienna Blackford (4)
Manorcroft Primary School, Egham

Carson-James' First Riddle

What could it be?
Follow the clues and see.

It looks like **a sandcastle**.
It sounds like **sprinkles**.
It smells like **a hot kettle**.
It feels like **soft balls.**
It tastes like **little balls**.

Have you guessed what it could be?
Look below and you will see,
It is...

Answer: **Sand**.

Carson-James Walsh (5)
Mengham Infant School, Hayling Island

Angel's First Riddle

What could it be?
Follow the clues and see.

It looks like **a pear**.
It sounds like ***ssss***.
It smells **good**.
It feels like **a flower**.
It tastes like **an apple**.

Have you guessed what it could be?
Look below and you will see,
It is...

Answer: **Grass**.

Angel Michael Bays (5)
Mengham Infant School, Hayling Island

Nathan's First Riddle

What could it be?
Follow the clues and see.

It looks like **a rectangle**.
It sounds like ***brmm.***
It smells like **rubber**.
It feels **hard**.
It tastes like **it**.

Have you guessed what it could be?
Look below and you will see,
It is...

Answer: **A car.**

Nathan (ZiYou) Li (4)
Mengham Infant School, Hayling Island

Kaushal's First Riddle

What could it be?
Follow the clues and see.

It looks like **a ball**.
It sounds **squishy**.
It smells like **vanilla**.
It feels like **lip balm**.
It tastes like **lip balm**.

Have you guessed what it could be?
Look below and you will see,
It is...

Answer: **A marshmallow.**

Kaushal Khatiwada (5)
Mengham Infant School, Hayling Island

Jacob's First Riddle

What could it be?
Follow the clues and see.

It looks like **pepper**.
It sounds **crunchy**.
It smells like **rotten pears**.
It feels like **snow**.
It tastes like **rotten oranges**.

Have you guessed what it could be?
Look below and you will see,
It is...

Answer: **Sand**.

Jacob Van Beers (4)
Mengham Infant School, Hayling Island

Eva's First Riddle

What could it be?
Follow the clues and see.

It looks **squishy**.
It sounds **squishy**.
It smells like **a strawberry.**
It feels **soft**.
It tastes like **a strawberry.**

Have you guessed what it could be?
Look below and you will see,
It is...

Answer: **A marshmallow.**

Eva Macias (4)
Mengham Infant School, Hayling Island

Livvy's First Riddle

What could it be?
Follow the clues and see.

It looks **sweet**.
It sounds **crunchy**.
It smells like **a strawberry**.
It feels **soft**.
It tastes like **a strawberry**.

Have you guessed what it could be?
Look below and you will see,
It is...

Answer: **A marshmallow.**

Livvy Moss (4)
Mengham Infant School, Hayling Island

Sinah's First Riddle

What could it be?
Follow the clues and see.

It looks like **a mountain**.
It sounds **squishy**.
It smells like **vanilla**.
It feels **soft**.
It tastes like **vanilla**.

Have you guessed what it could be?
Look below and you will see,
It is...

Answer: **A marshmallow.**

Sinah Lilly Cole (5)
Mengham Infant School, Hayling Island

Anna's First Riddle

What could it be?
Follow the clues and see.

It looks **hard**.
It sounds like **a rattle**.
It smells like **grass**.
It feels like **a chain**.
It tastes like **strawberries**.

Have you guessed what it could be?
Look below and you will see,
It is...

Answer: **A stone.**

Anna Nixon (4)
Mengham Infant School, Hayling Island

Sophia's First Riddle

What could it be?
Follow the clues and see.

It looks like **a mountain**.
It sounds **squishy**.
It smells like **lip balm**.
It feels **squishy**.
It tastes **yummy**.

Have you guessed what it could be?
Look below and you will see,
It is...

Answer: **A marshmallow.**

Sophia Marie Young (4)
Mengham Infant School, Hayling Island

Lowenna's First Riddle

What could it be?
Follow the clues and see.

It looks like **salt**.
It sounds like **a pom-pom**.
It smells like **sheep's wool**.
It feels **soft**.
It tastes **crunchy**.

Have you guessed what it could be?
Look below and you will see,
It is...

Answer: **Sand**.

Lowenna Marks (4)
Mengham Infant School, Hayling Island

Lily's First Riddle

What could it be?
Follow the clues and see.

It looks **colourful**.
It sounds like **a chirp**.
It smells like **meat and fur**.
It feels **furry**.
It tastes like **meat**.

Have you guessed what it could be?
Look below and you will see,
It is...

Answer: **A bird**.

Lily Beatrice Susan Butler (4)
Mengham Infant School, Hayling Island

Sienna's First Riddle

What could it be?
Follow the clues and see.

It looks like **powder**.
It sounds like **a zebra**.
It smells like **paint**.
It feels **crunchy**.
It tastes like **sparkles**.

Have you guessed what it could be?
Look below and you will see,
It is...

Answer: **Sand**.

Sienna Watson-Fraser (4)
Mengham Infant School, Hayling Island

Charlie's First Riddle

What could it be?
Follow the clues and see.

It looks like **corn on the cob**.
It sounds like **shaking**.
It smells like **grass**.
It feels **soft**.
It tastes **yucky**.

Have you guessed what it could be?
Look below and you will see,
It is...

Answer: **Sand**.

Charlie Hoare (4)
Mengham Infant School, Hayling Island

Zachary's First Riddle

What could it be?
Follow the clues and see.

It looks **blue**.
It sounds like ***swish.***
It smells like **pepper**.
It feels **bumpy**.
It tastes like **meat**.

Have you guessed what it could be?
Look below and you will see,
It is...

Answer: ***A fish.***

Zachary Austin House (4)
Mengham Infant School, Hayling Island

Jack's First Riddle

What could it be?
Follow the clues and see.

It looks like **a lightsaber**.
It sounds like **a stick.**
It smells like **dirt**.
It feels **hard**.
It tastes **yucky**.

Have you guessed what it could be?
Look below and you will see,
It is...

Answer: **A stick.**

Jack Clarke (4)
Mengham Infant School, Hayling Island

Gracie's First Riddle

What could it be?
Follow the clues and see.

It looks like **chocolate ice cream.**
It sounds **gentle**.
It smells like **a pen.**
It feels **soft.**
It tastes **yucky**.

Have you guessed what it could be?
Look below and you will see,
It is...

Answer: **Sand.**

Gracie Dawn Alison Heppell (4)
Mengham Infant School, Hayling Island

Isabelle's First Riddle

What could it be?
Follow the clues and see.

It looks like **chocolate**.
It sounds **soft**.
It smells like **a rotten banana**.
It feels **crunchy**.
It tastes **sour**.

Have you guessed what it could be?
Look below and you will see,
It is...

Answer: **Sand**.

Isabelle Bryne (5)
Mengham Infant School, Hayling Island

Amelia's First Riddle

What could it be?
Follow the clues and see.

It looks like **jelly**.
It sounds **crunchy**.
It smells like **apples**.
It feels like **pasta**.
It tastes like **sand**.

Have you guessed what it could be?
Look below and you will see,
It is...

Answer: **Grass**.

Amelia Angel Bugg (5)
Mengham Infant School, Hayling Island

Eva's First Riddle

What could it be?
Follow the clues and see.

It looks **thin**.
It sounds like **a phone**.
It smells like **strawberries**.
It feels **wet**.
It tastes like **apples**.

Have you guessed what it could be?
Look below and you will see,
It is...

Answer: **Grass**.

Eva Annabel Ekiri Ekomo (5)
Mengham Infant School, Hayling Island

Sadie's First Riddle

What could it be?
Follow the clues and see.

It looks **colourful**.
It sounds **noisy**.
It smells **fluttery**.
It feels **soft**.
It tastes like **wings**.

Have you guessed what it could be?
Look below and you will see,
It is...

Answer: A **butterfly**.

Sadie Wickens (4)
Mengham Infant School, Hayling Island

Harry's First Riddle

What could it be?
Follow the clues and see.

It looks **blue**.
It sounds like **a volcano**.
It smells **wet**.
It feels **rubbery**.
It tastes like **a nut**.

Have you guessed what it could be?
Look below and you will see,
It is...

Answer: **A whale**.

Harry Townsend (4)
Mengham Infant School, Hayling Island

Tina's First Riddle

What could it be?
Follow the clues and see.

It looks **hard**.
It sounds like **a harp**.
It smells like **sand**.
It feels **soft**.
It tastes **yucky**.

Have you guessed what it could be?
Look below and you will see,
It is...

Answer: ***A multi-link.***

Tina Wynne (5)
Mengham Infant School, Hayling Island

Lilli-Mai's First Riddle

What could it be?
Follow the clues and see.

It looks **squishy**.
It sounds **crunchy**.
It smells **nice**.
It feels **soft**.
It tastes **tasty**.

Have you guessed what it could be?
Look below and you will see,
It is...

Answer: **A marshmallow.**

Lilli-Mai Freeman (5)
Mengham Infant School, Hayling Island

Our First Riddle

What could it be?
Follow the clues and see.

It looks **black.**
It sounds **scary.**
It smells like **fire.**
It feels **hard.**
It tastes like **rock.**

Have you guessed what it could be?
Look below and you will see,
It is...

Answer: **A dragon.**

Hallie Hunter Keen (4), Kai Johnson Reid-Taylor (5), Raymond James Kerrin (4), Megan & Elisa
Mengham Infant School, Hayling Island

Bella's First Riddle

What could it be?
Follow the clues and see.

It looks **brown**.
It sounds **shaky**.
It smells **rotten**.
It feels **cold**.
It tastes like **ice cream**.

Have you guessed what it could be?
Look below and you will see,
It is...

Answer: **Sand**.

Bella Harrop (4)
Mengham Infant School, Hayling Island

Frankie's First Riddle

What could it be?
Follow the clues and see.

It looks **grey**.
It sounds **noisy**.
It smells like **mud**.
It feels **soft**.
It tastes **greasy**.

Have you guessed what it could be?
Look below and you will see,
It is...

Answer: **A hippo**.

Frankie John James Walker (4)
Mengham Infant School, Hayling Island

Harry's First Riddle

What could it be?
Follow the clues and see.

It looks **big**.
It smells like **a flower**.
It tastes like **a tomato**.

Have you guessed what it could be?
Look below and you will see,
It is...

Answer: **A paintbrush.**

Harry Lintott (4)
Mengham Infant School, Hayling Island

Cody's First Riddle

What could it be?
Follow the clues and see.

It looks **red and blue**.
It sounds like ***vroom, vroom, beep, beep***.
It smells like **petrol**.
It feels like **metal**.
It tastes like **an apple**.

Have you guessed what it could be?
Look below and you will see,
It is...

Answer: **A car.**

Cody Nilsson Harrison (4)

New Marston Primary School, Oxford

Lillian's First Riddle

What could it be?
Follow the clues and see.

It looks like **the sun**.
It sounds like **thunder**.
It smells like **something sour**.
It feels **furry**.
It tastes **bloody**.

Have you guessed what it could be?
Look below and you will see,
It is...

Answer: **A lion**.

Lillian Elizabeth Eileen Platt (5)
New Marston Primary School, Oxford

Yousef's First Riddle

What could it be?
Follow the clues and see.

It looks like **a potato**.
It sounds like **a roar**.
It smells like **a bin**.
It feels **hot**.
It tastes like **meat**.

Have you guessed what it could be?
Look below and you will see,
It is...

Answer: **A dinosaur.**

Yousef Janahi (5)
New Marston Primary School, Oxford

Brooke-Amelia's First Riddle

What could it be?
Follow the clues and see.

It looks **flat**.
It sounds like **breaking toys**.
It smells like **cheese**.
It feels **dry**.
It tastes like **cheese**.

Have you guessed what it could be?
Look below and you will see,
It is...

Answer: **A cracker**.

Brooke-Amelia Veronica Dallimore (4)
New Marston Primary School, Oxford

Jacob's First Riddle

What could it be?
Follow the clues and see.

It looks like **a giant bird**.
It sounds like **a big engine**.
It smells like **metal**.
It feels **very strong**.
It tastes like **a blue ice lolly**.

Have you guessed what it could be?
Look below and you will see,
It is...

Answer: **An aeroplane**.

Jacob Robbie Head (5)

Purley CE Primary School, Purley On Thames

Poppy's First Riddle

What could it be?
Follow the clues and see.

It looks like **a ball of fire.**
It sounds like ***sizzle.***
It smells like **fire.**
It feels **hot.**
It tastes like **strawberries.**

Have you guessed what it could be?
Look below and you will see,
It is...

Answer: **The sun.**

Poppy Allum (4)
Purley CE Primary School, Purley On Thames

Freya's First Riddle

What could it be?
Follow the clues and see.

It looks like **a diamond**.
It sounds like **sparkles**.
It smells like **winter**.
It feels like **ice**.
It tastes like **water**.

Have you guessed what it could be?
Look below and you will see,
It is...

Answer: **A snowflake.**

Freya Beau Eldred (4)
Purley CE Primary School, Purley On Thames

Phoebe's First Riddle

What could it be?
Follow the clues and see.

It looks **white.**
It sounds **crunchy.**
It smells like **cold air.**
It feels **wet and freezing.**
It tastes like **cold water.**

Have you guessed what it could be?
Look below and you will see,
It is...

Answer: **Snow.**

Phoebe Tigwell (5)
Purley CE Primary School, Purley On Thames

Margaux's First Riddle

What could it be?
Follow the clues and see.

It looks **scaly**.
It sounds like **bubbles**.
It smells **stinky**.
It feels **slimy**.
It tastes like **salt**.

Have you guessed what it could be?
Look below and you will see,
It is...

Answer: ***A fish.***

Margaux Lewis (4)
Purley CE Primary School, Purley On Thames

Cora's First Riddle

What could it be?
Follow the clues and see.

It looks **white**.
It sounds **squeaky**.
It smells like **a carrot**.
It feels **soft**.
It tastes **urgh**.

Have you guessed what it could be?
Look below and you will see,
It is...

Answer: **A rabbit.**

Cora Ham (4)
Purley CE Primary School, Purley On Thames

Phoebe's First Riddle

What could it be?
Follow the clues and see.

It looks like **a horse.**
It sounds like **a neigh.**
It smells like **sweet hay.**
It feels **soft and furry.**

Have you guessed what it could be?
Look below and you will see,
It is...

Answer: **A pony.**

Phoebe Tovey (4)
Purley CE Primary School, Purley On Thames

Rose's First Riddle

What could it be?
Follow the clues and see.

It looks like **a bouncy castle.**
It sounds like **cool music.**
It smells like **delicious party food.**
It feels like **the best day ever.**
It tastes like **chocolate cake.**

Have you guessed what it could be?
Look below and you will see,
It is...

Answer: **My birthday party.**

Rose Weller (5)
Queen Emma's Primary School, Witney

William's First Riddle

What could it be?
Follow the clues and see.

It looks like **an orange rectangle.**
It sounds like **a frying pan.**
It smells like **fantastic fish.**
It feels **crunchy on the outside.**
It tastes **fluffy and yummy.**

Have you guessed what it could be?
Look below and you will see,
It is...

Answer: **A fish finger.**

William Robert Leslie Thomas Acaster (5)
Queen Emma's Primary School, Witney

Noah's First Riddle

What could it be?
Follow the clues and see.

It looks like **a green field.**
It sounds like **cheering fans.**
It smells like **a smelly football kit.**
It feels like **slippy grass.**
It tastes like **cold air.**

Have you guessed what it could be?
Look below and you will see,
It is...

Answer: ***A football match.***

Noah George Houghton (4)
Queen Emma's Primary School, Witney

Sammy's First Riddle

What could it be?
Follow the clues and see.

It looks like **a tower of yumminess.**
It sounds like **crackling cheese.**
It smells like **yummy beef.**
It feels like **soft bread.**
It tastes like **my favourite food.**

Have you guessed what it could be?
Look below and you will see,
It is...

Answer: **A burger.**

Sammy Conway (5)
Queen Emma's Primary School, Witney

John's First Riddle

What could it be?
Follow the clues and see.

It looks like **a white rectangle.**
It sounds like **baby's music.**
It smells like **Mummy's cooking.**
It feels **nice and warm.**
It tastes like **yummy food.**

Have you guessed what it could be?
Look below and you will see,
It is...

Answer: **My house.**

John Anthony Eatson (4)
Queen Emma's Primary School, Witney

Jessie's First Riddle

What could it be?
Follow the clues and see.

It looks like **pretty presents.**
It sounds like **snapping crackers.**
It smells like **magic.**
It feels like **the best day.**
It tastes like **chocolate cake.**

Have you guessed what it could be?
Look below and you will see,
It is...

Answer: Christmas Day.

Jessie Potter de Castro (4)
Queen Emma's Primary School, Witney

Jacob's First Riddle

What could it be?
Follow the clues and see.

It looks like **a yummy treat.**
It sounds like **a noisy machine.**
It smells like **bubblegum.**
It feels like **a scratchy cone.**
It tastes like **cold sweets.**

Have you guessed what it could be?
Look below and you will see,
It is...

Answer: **Ice cream.**

Jacob Clayton (4)
Queen Emma's Primary School, Witney

Aslam's First Riddle

What could it be?
Follow the clues and see.

It looks like **a circle and it's pretty**.
It sounds like ***crunch***.
It smells like **a strawberry**.
It feels **hard**.
It tastes **yummy**.

Have you guessed what it could be?
Look below and you will see,
It is...

Answer: **A lollipop**.

Aslam Semlali (4)
Queen Emma's Primary School, Witney

Julia's First Riddle

What could it be?
Follow the clues and see.

It looks like **shapes**.
It sounds like ***crunch, crunch***.
It smells like **chicken**.
It feels **hard**.
It tastes **salty**.

Have you guessed what it could be?
Look below and you will see,
It is...

Answer: **A packet of chicken crisps.**

Julia Kaczorowska (4)
Queen Emma's Primary School, Witney

Noah's First Riddle

What could it be?
Follow the clues and see.

It looks like **brown squares.**
It sounds like ***snap, snap.***
It smells **nice.**
It feels **gooey.**
It tastes **yummy.**

Have you guessed what it could be?
Look below and you will see,
It is...

Answer: ***A bar of chocolate.***

Noah George Alfie Smith (4)
Queen Emma's Primary School, Witney

Ryan's First Riddle

What could it be?
Follow the clues and see.

It looks like **a circle**.
It sounds like ***boing, boing***.
It smells like **grass**.
It feels **hard**.
It tastes like **mud, yuck**.

Have you guessed what it could be?
Look below and you will see,
It is...

Answer: **A football**.

Ryan Peter Olive (4)

Queen Emma's Primary School, Witney

Taylor's First Riddle

What could it be?
Follow the clues and see.

It looks like **rectangles**.
It sounds **crispy**.
It smells like **wheat on the farm.**
It feels like **straw**.
It tastes **yummy**.

Have you guessed what it could be?
Look below and you will see,
It is...

*Answer: **Weetabix**.*

Taylor William Newport (4)
Queen Emma's Primary School, Witney

Harry's First Riddle

What could it be?
Follow the clues and see.

It looks like **fluffy clouds**.
It sounds **crunchy**.
It smells like **toffee**.
It feels **knobbly**.
It tastes like **sweet**.

Have you guessed what it could be?
Look below and you will see,
It is...

Answer: **Popcorn**.

Harry Challender (4)
Queen Emma's Primary School, Witney

Tahiya's First Riddle

What could it be?
Follow the clues and see.

It looks **wavy**.
It sounds like ***splish-splash***.
It smells like **seaweed**.
It feels **cold**.
It tastes **salty**.

Have you guessed what it could be?
Look below and you will see,
It is...

Answer: ***The sea.***

Tahiya Ahmed (4)
Queen Emma's Primary School, Witney

Holly's First Riddle

This is my riddle about an amazing animal.
What could it be?
Follow the clues to see!

This animal has **lots of thick fur** on its body,
And its colour is **black and gold and yellow**.
This animal has **four furry paws for** feet,
It likes **its prey and fresh meat** to eat.
The grasslands and the forests is where it lives,
Its favourite things to do are **hunt for food and climb trees**.
This animal has **two big** ears,
It makes **loud grr** sounds for you to hear.

Are you an animal whizz?
Have you guessed what it is?
It is...

Answer: **A leopard.**

Holly Tierney (7)
St Francis Catholic Primary School, Ascot

Isabelle's First Riddle

This is my riddle about an amazing animal.
What could it be?
Follow the clues to see!

This animal has **fluffy short fur spotted with dots** on its body,
And its colour is **yellow and brown with black spots.**
This animal has **a face with black tear marks, nice long legs and four round, clawed** feet,
It likes **freshly caught animal meat** to eat.
In a dry, brown grassland is where it lives,
Its favourite thing to do is **run amazingly fast.**
This animal has **fuzzy semicircle** ears,
It makes **loud purring** sounds for you to hear.

Are you an animal whizz?
Have you guessed what it is?
It is...

Answer: **A cheetah.**

Isabelle R (7)

St Francis Catholic Primary School, Ascot

Austin's First Riddle

This is my riddle about an amazing animal.
What could it be?
Follow the clues to see!

This animal has **furry fur** on its body,
And its colour is **black with a big grey stripe with a white line on its back.**
This animal has **four long, clawed** feet,
It likes **gooey honey and reptiles** to eat.
South Africa is where it lives,
Its favourite thing to do is **use its brain and get up to mischief**.
This animal has **two hidden** ears,
It makes **loud scratching** sounds for you to hear.

Are you an animal whizz?
Have you guessed what it is?

It is...

Answer: **A honey badger.**

Austin David MacNeill (6)
St Francis Catholic Primary School, Ascot

Amelie's First Riddle

This is my riddle about an amazing animal.
What could it be?
Follow the clues to see!

This animal has **fantastic scales** on its body,
And its colour is **a glorious green with yellow stripes**.
This animal has **a long tail and no arms and no** feet,
It likes **frogs, mice and eggs** to eat.
In a dark forest is where it lives,
Its favourite thing to do is **smell with its tongue**.
This animal has **two hidden** ears,
It makes **long sss** sounds for you to hear.

Are you an animal whizz?
Have you guessed what it is?

It is...

Answer: **A snake.**

Amelie Rose O'Donnell (7)

St Francis Catholic Primary School, Ascot

Savana's First Riddle

This is my riddle about an amazing animal.
What could it be?
Follow the clues to see!

This animal has **fascinating fuzzy fur** on its body,
And its colour is **really dark brown and white**.
This animal has **four jumpy legs with such cute** feet,
It likes **raw vegetables and fresh grass** to eat.
In the dark woods is where it lives,
Its favourite thing to do is **hop all around**.
This animal has **fantastically long** ears,
It makes **small nibbling** sounds for you to hear.

Are you an animal whizz?
Have you guessed what it is?

It is...

Answer: A bunny.

Savana-Marie Lorraine (7)
St Francis Catholic Primary School, Ascot

James' First Riddle

This is my riddle about an amazing animal.
What could it be?
Follow the clues to see!

This animal has **fluttering feathers** on its body,
And its colour is **gorgeous golden and brown.**
This animal has **strong talons on its** feet,
It likes **little insects to eat and little birds** to eat.
The forest is where it lives,
Its favourite thing to do is **rest and fight and fly.**
This animal has **two pointy** ears,
It makes **cheep** sounds for you to hear.

Are you an animal whizz?
Have you guessed what it is?

It is...

Answer: A golden eagle.

James Foster (6)
St Francis Catholic Primary School, Ascot

Hari K M's First Riddle

This is my riddle about an amazing animal.
What could it be?
Follow the clues to see!

This animal has **long feathers** on its body,
And its colour is **grey, brown and white.**
This animal has **funny chicken** feet,
It likes **insects and especially worms** to eat.
On a scary island is where it lives,
Its favourite thing to do is **fly around and look for worms.**
This animal has **very good hidden** ears,
It makes **pigeon** sounds for you to hear.

Are you an animal whizz?
Have you guessed what it is?
It is...

Answer: **A dodo bird.**

Hari K M (6)
St Francis Catholic Primary School, Ascot

Daisy's First Riddle

This is my riddle about an amazing animal.
What could it be?
Follow the clues to see!

This animal has **smooth scales** on its body,
And its colour is **jade with aquamarine dots on it**.
This animal has **a thin tail and no** feet,
It likes **fresh meat** to eat.
In the deep dark forest is where it lives,
Its favourite thing to do is **slither in the forest**.
This animal has **a crystal head but no** ears,
It makes **hissing** sounds for you to hear.

Are you an animal whizz?
Have you guessed what it is?
It is...

Answer: **A snake.**

Daisy E (6)
St Francis Catholic Primary School, Ascot

Emily's First Riddle

This is my riddle about an amazing animal.
What could it be?
Follow the clues to see!

This animal has **smooth scales** on its body,
And its colour is **dull green with yellow dots.**
This animal has **a tongue to test food and zero** feet,
It likes **squished mice** to eat.
In a really hot desert is where it lives,
Its favourite thing to do is **hunt for other animals.**
This animal has **no** ears,
It makes **hissing** sounds for you to hear.

Are you an animal whizz?
Have you guessed what it is?
It is...

Answer: **A snake.**

Emily W (6)
St Francis Catholic Primary School, Ascot

Harry's First Riddle

This is my riddle about an amazing animal.
What could it be?
Follow the clues to see!

This animal has **brown feathers** on its body,
And its colour is **shaded browny, goldy**.
This animal has **three-clawed** feet,
It likes **fresh fish and wiggly worms** to eat.
In a nest on a mountain is where it lives,
Its favourite thing to do is **fly and swoop**.
This animal has **hidden** ears,
It makes **screeching** sounds for you to hear.

Are you an animal whizz?
Have you guessed what it is?
It is...

Answer: **A golden eagle.**

Harry Anderson (6)
St Francis Catholic Primary School, Ascot

James' First Riddle

This is my riddle about an amazing animal.
What could it be?
Follow the clues to see!

This animal has **rubbery, bumpy skin** on its body,
And its colour is **dark grey**.
This animal has **sharp teeth and fins for feet**,
It likes **fresh fish** to eat.
In the sea is where it lives,
Its favourite thing to do is **swim and hunt for food**.
This animal has **not got** ears,
It makes **chomping** sounds for you to hear.

Are you an animal whizz?
Have you guessed what it is?

It is...

Answer: **A hammerhead shark.**

James Gonzales (7)
St Francis Catholic Primary School, Ascot

Mervin's First Riddle

This is my riddle about an amazing animal.
What could it be?
Follow the clues to see!

This animal has **really soft fur** on its body,
And its colour is **golden yellow.**
This animal has **four strong** feet,
It likes **lots of meat** to eat.
Sunny grasslands in Africa is where it lives,
Its favourite thing to do is **hunt and run fast.**
This animal has **soft, big** ears,
It makes **loud roaring** sounds for you to
hear.

Are you an animal whizz?
Have you guessed what it is?
It is...

Answer: **A lion.**

Mervin Manish (6)
St Francis Catholic Primary School, Ascot

Charlie's First Riddle

This is my riddle about an amazing animal.
What could it be?
Follow the clues to see!

This animal has **lots of soft fur** on its body,
And its colour is **yellow and big black spots.**
This animal has **four big soft** feet,
It likes **leftover meat** to eat.
In Africa is where it lives,
Its favourite thing to do is **run and eat.**
This animal has **big** ears,
It makes **a noise like someone laughing** for
you to hear.

Are you an animal whizz?
Have you guessed what it is?
It is...

Answer: **A hyena.**

Charlie W (6)
St Francis Catholic Primary School, Ascot

Martha's First Riddle

This is my riddle about an amazing animal.
What could it be?
Follow the clues to see!

This animal has **soft fur** on its body,
And its colour is **light brown**.
This animal has **two arms and two human** feet,
It likes **fresh fruit** to eat.
In the wild forest is where it lives,
Its favourite thing to do is **swing in the trees.**
This animal has **two** ears,
It makes **ooh oooh ooh** sounds for you to hear.

Are you an animal whizz?
Have you guessed what it is?

It is...

Answer: **A monkey.**

Martha Ann MacNeill (6)
St Francis Catholic Primary School, Ascot

Bailey's First Riddle

This is my riddle about an amazing animal.
What could it be?
Follow the clues to see!

This animal has **light grey skin** on its body,
And its colour is **light grey**.
This animal has **one tail and four** feet,
It likes **dry grass** to eat.
Africa is where it lives,
Its favourite thing to do is **eat grass all day**.
This animal has **rough skin and** ears,
It makes **baby elephant** sounds for you to hear.

Are you an animal whizz?
Have you guessed what it is?
It is...

Answer: **A white rhino.**

Bailey A (7)
St Francis Catholic Primary School, Ascot

Isabelle's First Riddle

This is my riddle about an amazing animal.
What could it be?
Follow the clues to see!

This animal has **fuzzy, rough fur** on its body,
And its colour is **yellow like sand**.
This animal has **four flat** feet,
It likes **green leaves** to eat.
In a desert is where it lives,
Its favourite thing to do is **be ridden by people**.
This animal has **two** ears,
It makes **mooing and growling** sounds for you to hear.

Are you an animal whizz?
Have you guessed what it is?
It is...

Answer: **A camel**.

Isabelle T G (6)
St Francis Catholic Primary School, Ascot

Kiara's First Riddle

This is my riddle about an amazing animal.
What could it be?
Follow the clues to see!

This animal has **super thick fur** on its body,
And its colour is **bronze and brown.**
This animal has **furry** feet,
It likes **fresh fruit** to eat.
In a tree in a forest is where it lives,
Its favourite thing to do is **swing.**
This animal has **two fluffy** ears,
It makes **ooh ooh aah** sounds for you to hear.

Are you an animal whizz?
Have you guessed what it is?
It is...

Answer: ***A monkey.***

Kiara Byles (6)
St Francis Catholic Primary School, Ascot

Sophia's First Riddle

This is my riddle about an amazing animal.
What could it be?
Follow the clues to see!

This animal has **a furry coat** on its body,
And its colour is **orange**.
This animal has **hard** feet,
It likes **green grass** to eat.
In a green meadow is where it lives,
Its favourite thing to do is **run fast like a cheetah**.
This animal has **two pointy** ears,
It makes **soft bprr** sounds for you to hear.

Are you an animal whizz?
Have you guessed what it is?
It is...

Answer: **A horse**.

Sophia F (6)
St Francis Catholic Primary School, Ascot

Archie's First Riddle

This is my riddle about an amazing animal.
What could it be?
Follow the clues to see!

This animal has **soft fur** on its body,
And its colour is **brown and peach**.
This animal has **pads on its** feet,
It likes **yellow bananas** to eat.
In a jungle is where it lives,
Its favourite thing to do is **swing on vines**.
This animal has **fluffy** ears,
It makes **oo oo aa** sounds for you to hear.

Are you an animal whizz?
Have you guessed what it is?
It is...

Answer: **A monkey.**

Archie Bird (7)
St Francis Catholic Primary School, Ascot

Harry's First Riddle

This is my riddle about an amazing animal.
What could it be?
Follow the clues to see!

This animal has **soft fur** on its body,
And its colour is **orange and white**.
This animal has **four clawed** feet,
It likes **fresh meat** to eat.
The jungle is where it lives,
Its favourite things to do are **eat meat and swim**.
This animal has **fluffy** ears,
It makes **grrr** sounds for you to hear.

Are you an animal whizz?
Have you guessed what it is?
It is...

Answer: **A tiger**.

Harry W (7)
St Francis Catholic Primary School, Ascot

Scott's First Riddle

This is my riddle about an amazing animal.
What could it be?
Follow the clues to see!

This animal has **shiny fur** on its body,
And its colour is **shiny black.**
This animal has **hooves for** feet,
It likes **long grass** to eat.
Africa is where it lives,
Its favourite thing to do is **charge at people**.
This animal has **floppy** ears,
It makes **moo** sounds for you to hear.

Are you an animal whizz?
Have you guessed what it is?
It is...

Answer: ***A buffalo.***

Scott Borthwick (6)
St Francis Catholic Primary School, Ascot

James' First Riddle

This is my riddle about an amazing animal.
What could it be?
Follow the clues to see!

This animal has **scales** on its body,
And its colour is **green and peach**.
This animal has **no** feet,
It likes **little animals** to eat.
Africa is where it lives,
Its favourite thing to do is **slither**.
This animal has **no** ears,
It makes **hiss hiss** sounds for you to hear.

Are you an animal whizz?
Have you guessed what it is?
It is...

Answer: **A snake.**

James C (6)
St Francis Catholic Primary School, Ascot

Kyle's First Riddle

What could it be?
Follow the clues and see.

It looks like **a little man.**
It sounds like **run, run.**
It smells like **ginger and spices.**
It feels like **a little bit of bread.**
It tastes like **I want some more.**

Have you guessed what it could be?
Look below and you will see,
It is...

Answer: ***A gingerbread man biscuit.***

Kyle Grant Kohler (4)
St Michael's CE Primary School, Sunninghill

Scarlett's First Riddle

What could it be?
Follow the clues and see.

It looks like **a marshmallow rainbow.**
It sounds like **a horse - *neigh*.**
It smells like **sweeties.**
It feels like **soft fur.**
It tastes like **candyfloss.**

Have you guessed what it could be?
Look below and you will see,
It is...

Answer: **A unicorn.**

Scarlett Vaughan (4)
St Michael's CE Primary School, Sunninghill

Arabella's First Riddle

What could it be?
Follow the clues and see.

It looks like **a long body and wings.**
It sounds like ***tweet, tweet.***
It smells like **fresh air.**
It feels like **a soft blanket.**
It tastes like **feathers.**

Have you guessed what it could be?
Look below and you will see,
It is...

*Answer: **A bird.***

Arabella Bristow (4)
St Michael's CE Primary School, Sunninghill

Henry's First Riddle

What could it be?
Follow the clues and see.

It looks like **a ladder, wavy and long.**
It sounds **chewy.**
It smells like **chocolate.**
It feels **squashy and hard.**
It tastes like **caramel and chocolate.**

Have you guessed what it could be?
Look below and you will see,
It is...

Answer: **A Curly Wurly.**

Henry Beacham (5)
St Michael's CE Primary School, Sunninghill

Sophie's First Riddle

What could it be?
Follow the clues and see.

It looks like **a ball with a hump.**
It sounds like ***pop.***
It smells like **a rubber.**
It feels like **an elastic band.**
It tastes like **a rubber.**

Have you guessed what it could be?
Look below and you will see,
It is...

Answer: **A balloon.**

Sophie O'Neill (4)
St Michael's CE Primary School, Sunninghill

Daisy's First Riddle

What could it be?
Follow the clues and see.

It looks **red**.
It sounds like ***wobble***.
It smells like **a raspberry**.
It feels **squishy and cold**.
It tastes **slippery and sweet**.

Have you guessed what it could be?
Look below and you will see,
It is...

Answer: Jelly.

Daisy Cordes (5)
St Michael's CE Primary School, Sunninghill

Finn's First Riddle

What could it be?
Follow the clues and see.

It looks like **a dinosaur**.
It sounds like **a lion**.
It smells like **a toasted marshmallow**.
It feels like **a snake**.
It tastes like **sausages**.

Have you guessed what it could be?
Look below and you will see,
It is...

Answer: **A dragon**.

Finn Hilleard (4)
St Michael's CE Primary School, Sunninghill

Nina-Grae's First Riddle

What could it be?
Follow the clues and see.

It looks like **snow**.
It sounds like **licking ice**.
It smells **delicious**.
It feels like **soft ice**.
It tastes like **cold sweets**.

Have you guessed what it could be?
Look below and you will see,
It is...

Answer: **Ice cream**.

Nina-Grae Bold (5)
St Michael's CE Primary School, Sunninghill

Francesca's First Riddle

What could it be?
Follow the clues and see.

It looks like **snow**.
It sounds **crunchy**.
It smells like **water**.
It feels like **cold water**.
It tastes like **water**.

Have you guessed what it could be?
Look below and you will see,
It is...

Answer: **Ice**.

Francesca Monghan (4)
St Michael's CE Primary School, Sunninghill

Isaac's First Riddle

What could it be?
Follow the clues and see.

It looks like **pretty stars**.
It sounds like **a big bang**.
It smells like **a bonfire**.

Have you guessed what it could be?
Look below and you will see,
It is...

Answer: ***A firework.***

Isaac Read (4)
St Michael's CE Primary School, Sunninghill

Rafi's First Riddle

This is my riddle about an amazing animal.
What could it be?
Follow the clues to see!

This animal has **a big bump** on its head,
And its colour is **grey**.
This animal has **two** feet,
It likes **seeds and leaves** to eat.
The desert is where it lives,
Its favourite thing to do is **bash heads**.
This animal has **two** ears,
It makes ***ooooo*** sounds for you to hear.

Are you an animal whizz?
Have you guessed what it is?
It is...

Answer: **A pachycephalosaurus**.

Raphael Nikkhah (4)
Waddesdon Village Primary School, Waddesdon

Camilla's First Riddle

This is my riddle about an amazing animal.
What could it be?
Follow the clues to see!

This animal has **feathers** on its body,
And its colours are **green and grey**.
This animal has **two** feet,
It likes **lizards** to eat.
A sandy desert is where it lives,
Its favourite thing to do is **to hunt**.
This animal has **two** ears,
It makes ***rarrrrah*** sounds for you to hear.

Are you an animal whizz?
Have you guessed what it is?
It is...

Answer: **A velociraptor.**

Camilla Rose Hassard (5)
Waddesdon Village Primary School, Waddesdon

Akshaya's First Riddle

This is my riddle about an amazing animal.
What could it be?
Follow the clues to see!

This animal has **a tail** on its body,
And its colour is **green.**
This animal has **stomping** feet,
It likes **leaves and flowers** to eat.
The forest is where it lives,
Its favourite thing to do is **eat**.
This animal has **two** ears,
It makes ***rarrrrah*** sounds for you to hear.

Are you an animal whizz?
Have you guessed what it is?
It is...

Answer: **A brontosaurus.**

Akshaya Ravisangar (4)
Waddesdon Village Primary School, Waddesdon

Our First Riddle

This is my riddle about an amazing animal.
What could it be?
Follow the clues to see!

This animal has **wings** on its body,
And its colour is **grey**.
This animal has **two** feet,
It likes **fish** to eat.
In the trees are where it lives,
Its favourite thing to do is **fly**.
This animal has **two small** ears,
It makes **squawking** sounds for you to hear.

Are you an animal whizz?
Have you guessed what it is?
It is...

Answer: **A pterodactyl**.

Ayaan (4), Roman Fitzgerald (5), Parker McCann (5) & Muskaan Manji (5)
Waddesdon Village Primary School, Waddesdon

Haydn's & Amari's First Riddle

This is my riddle about an amazing animal.
What could it be?
Follow the clues to see!

This animal has **rough skin** on its body,
And its colour is **grey**.
This animal has **four** feet,
It likes **leaves** to eat.
The jungle is where it lives,
Its favourite thing is **being tall**.
This animal has **two** ears,
It makes **roaring** sounds for you to hear.

Are you an animal whizz?
Have you guessed what it is?
It is...

Answer: **A diplodocus**.

Haydn (4) & Amari (4)
Waddesdon Village Primary School, Waddesdon

Bella's First Riddle

This is my riddle about an amazing animal.
What could it be?
Follow the clues to see!

This animal has **fur** on its body,
And its colour is **brown.**
This animal has **four big** feet,
It likes **plants** to eat.
On the ice is where it lives,
Its favourite thing to do is **play with its friends**.
This animal has ears,
It makes ***mmmm*** sounds for you to hear.

Are you an animal whizz?
Have you guessed what it is?
It is...

Answer: ***A mammoth.***

Bella Matheou (5)
Waddesdon Village Primary School, Waddesdon

Sebastian's First Riddle

This is my riddle about an amazing animal.
What could it be?
Follow the clues to see!

This animal has **wings** on its body,
And its colour is **purple.**
This animal has **two** feet,
It likes **fish** to eat.
In the sky is where it lives,
Its favourite thing to do is **fly.**
This animal has **two** ears,
It makes **squawking** sounds for you to hear.

Are you an animal whizz?
Have you guessed what it is?
It is...

Answer: **A pterodactyl.**

Sebastian Green (5)
Waddesdon Village Primary School, Waddesdon

Our First Riddle

This is my riddle about an amazing animal.
What could it be?
Follow the clues to see!

This animal has **stripes** on its body,
And its colour is **green**.
This animal has **two** feet,
It likes **meat** to eat.
The jungle is where it lives,
Its favourite thing to do is **scare**.
This animal has **two** ears,
It makes **roaring** sounds for you to hear.

Are you an animal whizz?
Have you guessed what it is?
It is...

Answer: **A T-rex.**

Harriet Burke (4), Madison (5), Stewart & Esmee Boyt (4)
Waddesdon Village Primary School, Waddesdon

Our First Riddle

This is my riddle about a brilliant vehicle.
What could it be?
Follow the clues to see!

It has **no** wheels,
Super speed is the speed it goes.
Its colours are **black and brown**,
Fifty people can fit in it.
Gliding is how it moves,
People use it to **find treasure**.

Have you guessed what it could be?
Look below and you will see,
It is...

Answer: ***A pirate ship.***

Vinuri Patkirajage Don (4), Katrina, Phoebe & William Henderson (4)
Waddesdon Village Primary School, Waddesdon

Our First Riddle

This is my riddle about a brilliant vehicle.
What could it be?
Follow the clues to see!

It has **two** wheels,
Really fast is the speed it goes.
Its colour is **black**,
Two people can fit in it.
Roaring is how it moves,
People use it to go to **places**.

Have you guessed what it could be?
Look below and you will see,
It is...

Answer: **A motorbike.**

Jacob (4), Riley & Zainab (4)
Waddesdon Village Primary School, Waddesdon

Our First Riddle

This is my riddle about a brilliant vehicle.
What could it be?
Follow the clues to see!

It has **three** wheels,
Flashing speed is the speed it goes.
Its colour is **white**,
Lots of people can fit in it.
Flying is how it moves,
People use it to go **on holiday**.

Have you guessed what it could be?
Look below and you will see,
It is...

Answer: **An aeroplane.**

Kaeson (4), Phoebe Harrison (5) & James Conor Murnan (5)
Waddesdon Village Primary School, Waddesdon

Our First Riddle

What could it be?
Follow the clues and see.

It looks **tall and green.**
It sounds **swishy and swashy.**
It smells like **nuts.**
It feels **hard and bumpy.**
It tastes like **nature.**

Have you guessed what it could be?
Look below and you will see,
It is...

Answer: **A tree.**

Chloe Ainsworth (5), Phoebe & Reggie (4)
Waddesdon Village Primary School, Waddesdon

Stanley's First Riddle

What could it be?
Follow the clues and see.

It looks like **it used to belong to an animal.**
It sounds like **if you listen carefully you may hear the sea.**
It smells like **the seaside.**
It feels **hard, bumpy and smooth.**
It tastes **very salty.**

Have you guessed what it could be?
Look below and you will see,
It is...

Answer: **A seashell.**

Stanley Johnson (5)
Waterside Academy, Rowans

Joshua's First Riddle

What could it be?
Follow the clues and see.

It looks **fat, pink and oval**.
It sounds like ***honk, honk, honk***.
It smells **stinky**.
It feels **smooth and hairy**.
It tastes like **sausages**.

Have you guessed what it could be?
Look below and you will see,
It is...

Answer: **A pig**.

Joshua Bamgboye (5)
Waterside Academy, Rowans

Jack's First Riddle

What could it be?
Follow the clues and see.

It looks **white and medium-sized.**
It sounds like **a loud humming noise.**
It smells like **nothing.**
It feels **smooth and hard.**
It tastes like **nothing - probably dust.**

Have you guessed what it could be?
Look below and you will see,
It is...

Answer: **A Hoover.**

Jack Simon Howe (4)
Waterside Academy, Rowans

Leo's First Riddle

What could it be?
Follow the clues and see.

It looks like **a red and wobbly mess.**
It sounds like ***wobble, wobble.***
It smells like **nothing.**
It feels **slimy and cold.**
It tastes **strawberry flavoured.**

Have you guessed what it could be?
Look below and you will see,
It is...

Answer: Jelly.

Leo Warr (5)
Waterside Academy, Rowans

Harrison's First Riddle

What could it be?
Follow the clues and see.

It looks like **a fluffy rainbow.**
It sounds like **lots of happy whistles.**
It smells like **feathers.**
It feels like **soft silk.**
It tastes like **a bird.**

Have you guessed what it could be?
Look below and you will see,
It is...

Answer: **A parrot.**

Harrison Hurt (5)
Waterside Academy, Rowans

Maddison's First Riddle

What could it be?
Follow the clues and see.

It looks like **a horse**.
It sounds like **neigh**.
It smells like **cotton candy**.
It feels like **a furry blanket**.
It tastes like **ice cream**.

Have you guessed what it could be?
Look below and you will see,
It is...

Answer: **A unicorn**.

Maddison Lacey (5)
Waterside Academy, Rowans

Isabella's First Riddle

What could it be?
Follow the clues and see.

It looks like **water**.
It sounds like ***whoosh***.
It smells like **seaweed and fish**.
It feels like **nothing**.
It tastes like **salt**.

Have you guessed what it could be?
Look below and you will see,
It is...

Answer: **The sea.**

Isabella Draper (5)
Waterside Academy, Rowans

Ray's First Riddle

What could it be?
Follow the clues and see.

It looks like **a yellow planet**.
It sounds like **a drum**.
It smells like **rubber**.
It feels like **slime**.
It tastes like **plastic**.

Have you guessed what it could be?
Look below and you will see,
It is...

Answer: **A bouncy ball.**

Ray Ryan (4)
Waterside Academy, Rowans

Sofia's First Riddle

What could it be?
Follow the clues and see.

It looks like **a proper flower**.
It sounds like **nothing**.
It smells **really bad**.
It feels **soft**.
It tastes **bitter**.

Have you guessed what it could be?
Look below and you will see,
It is...

Answer: **A carnivorous plant.**

Sofia Ciortan (4)
Waterside Academy, Rowans

Ava's First Riddle

Who could it be?
Follow the clues and see.

She looks like **a lady**.
She sounds like **a fish**.
She smells like **the sea**.
She feels like **scales**.
She tastes like **seaweed**.

Have you guessed who it could be?
Look below and you will see,
It is...

Answer: **A mermaid**.

Ava Lily Robson (5)
Waterside Academy, Rowans

Ticiane's First Riddle

What could it be?
Follow the clues and see.

It looks like **a bird**.
It sounds like **a sea hawk.**
It smells like **fish.**
It feels like **wet rubber.**
It tastes like **fish.**

Have you guessed what it could be?
Look below and you will see,
It is...

Answer: **A penguin.**

Ticiane Sequeira (5)
Waterside Academy, Rowans

Maxwell's First Riddle

What could it be?
Follow the clues and see.

It looks **orange and black.**
It sounds like **'figer'. It roars!**
It smells **nice.**
It feels **soft.**
It tastes **fluffy.**

Have you guessed what it could be?
Look below and you will see,
It is...

Answer: **A tiger.**

Maxwell King (5)
Waterside Academy, Rowans

Aaron's First Riddle

What could it be?
Follow the clues and see.

It looks **green**.
It sounds like ***chomp.***
It smells like **the sea**.
It feels **spiky**.
It tastes like **water**.

Have you guessed what it could be?
Look below and you will see,
It is...

Answer: ***A crocodile.***

Aaron Kennedy (5)
Waterside Academy, Rowans

Zachary's First Riddle

What could it be?
Follow the clues and see.

It looks **white**.
It sounds like **the wind**.
It smells like **nothing**.
It feels like **ice**.
It tastes like **air**.

Have you guessed what it could be?
Look below and you will see,
It is...

Answer: **A ghost**.

Zachary Parry-Radway (5)
Waterside Academy, Rowans

Rachel's First Riddle

What could it be?
Follow the clues and see.

It looks like **a man.**
It smells like **ice.**
It feels like **a freezer.**
It tastes like **an ice cube.**

Have you guessed what it could be?
Look below and you will see,
It is...

Answer: **A snowman.**

Rachel Jemima Samuel (5)
Waterside Academy, Rowans

YOUNG WRITERS INFORMATION

We hope you have enjoyed reading this book – and that you will continue to in the coming years.

If you're a young writer who enjoys reading and creative writing, or the parent of an enthusiastic poet or story writer, do visit our website **www.youngwriters.co.uk**. Here you will find free competitions, workshops and games, as well as recommended reads, a poetry glossary and our blog. There's lots to keep budding writers motivated to write!

If you would like to order further copies of this book, or any of our other titles, then please give us a call or order via your online account.

Young Writers
Remus House
Coltsfoot Drive
Peterborough
PE2 9BF
(01733) 890066
info@youngwriters.co.uk

Join in the conversation!
Tips, news, giveaways and much more!

YoungWritersUK   @YoungWritersCW